AF255627

Heart Speaks

1: Heart Healing

poems and paintings by

Kathleen Quigley

Heart Speaks Press
Cambridge, Massachusetts 2020

Author photo: Karen Micciulla
Book design: Jonathan Weinert

Printed in the United States of America
First Edition

Library of Congress Control Number: 2020901084
ISBN 13: 978-0-578-63633-7

Heart Speaks Press
27 Grozier Road
Cambridge, MA 02138

kathleenquigley.com

Contents

1

♥

Heart Flowering

Universal Heart Poem
from the High Heart

Opening

Growing

Blossoming in Love

Plant your seed within the Earth of your Heart

Root Deeply

Love Abundantly

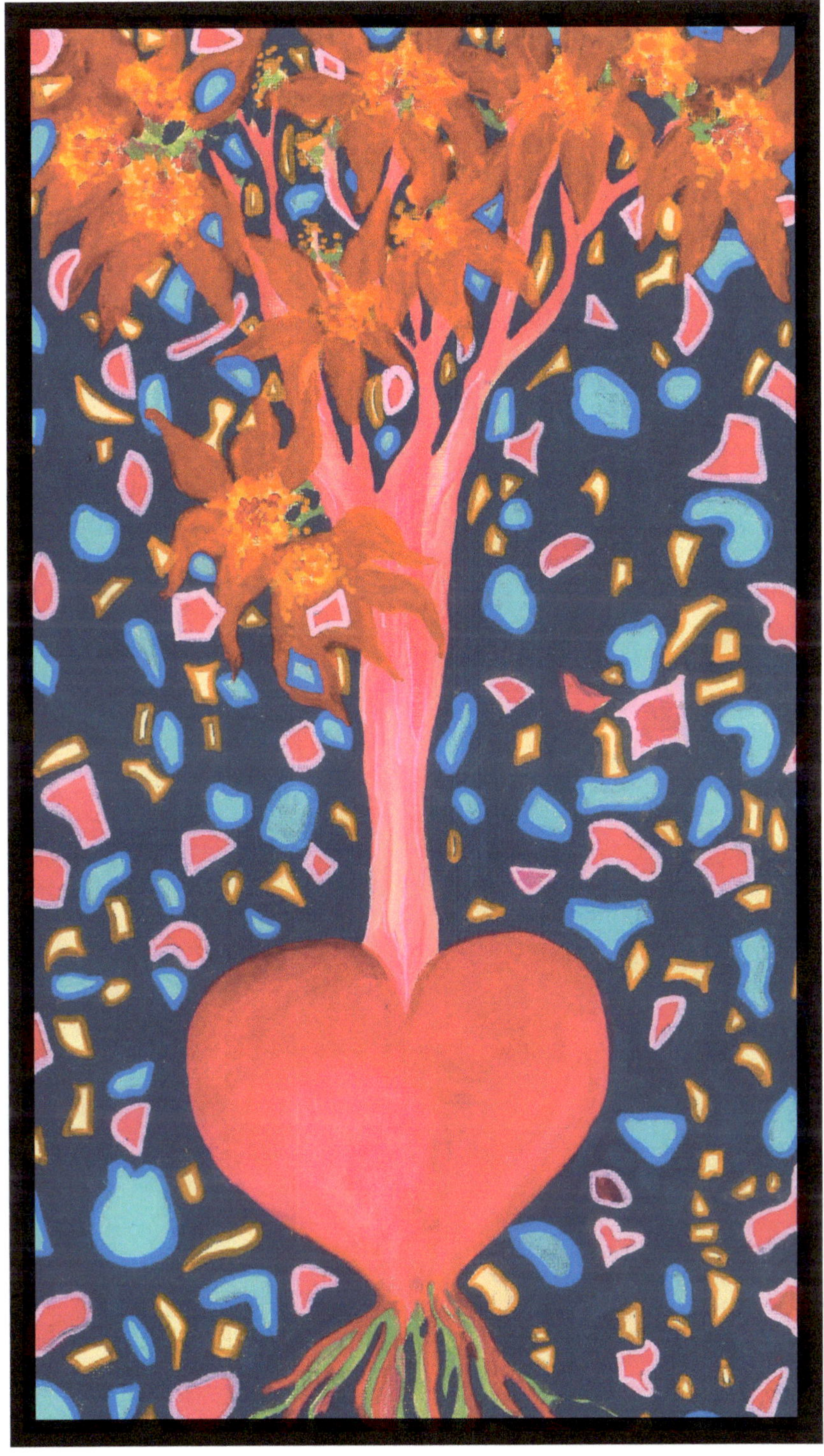

My Heart Wisdom

I AM the One who blooms into the heavens, each flower a star. I AM rooted into the Earth and I connect Heaven and Earth. I AM the connection. I AM where you connect to Heaven and Earth; In Me, Through Me, With Me. I am the deep love that sustains all. I AM beating. I AM alive. Know Me with all your hearts and know that you are ALIVE.

2

♥

Heart Tree of Life

Universal Heart Poem
from the High Heart

I AM the Tree of Life

Rooted in the beloved Mother Gia

Ascending into the beloved Father Sky

I bridge Heaven and Earth

I AM the Conduit

I AM the Vessel

BE ME

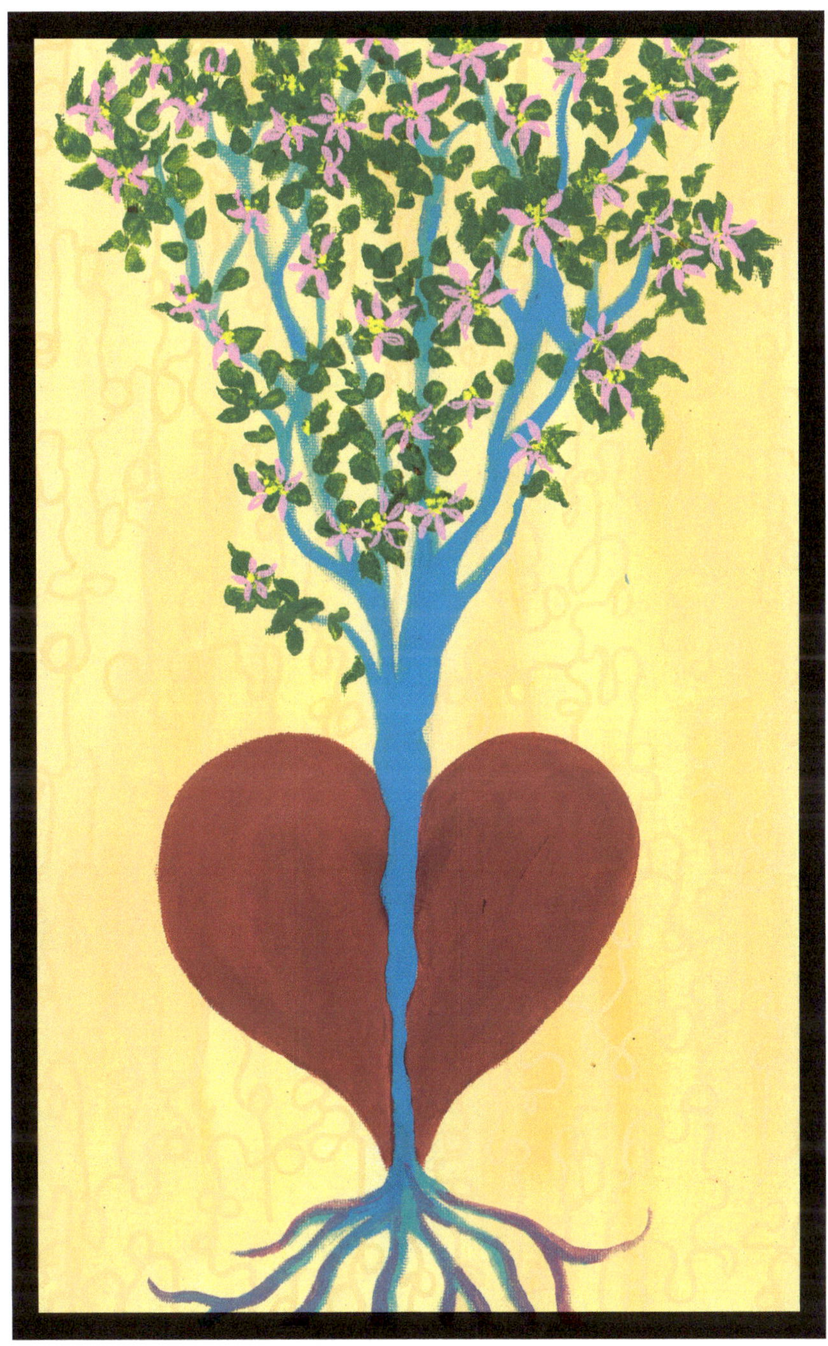

My Heart Wisdom

You are the tree of life. Each individual person is its own tree spanning and connecting the Earth with the Sky. Know Me in you when you look at a tree, it is a constant reminder of your true self. I AM the scared design of life. I AM the sacred conduit between Heaven and Earth. Stand tall in your Tree of Life. Know you are Tree. Root deeply into the Earth, drinking up all her sustenance and energy, filling your heart and continuing upward to Father Sky into the universal heavens. Feed the Earth, feed yourself, feed the Heavens. You are the life line. You are the scared conduit. Know it, Be it.

3

♥

Heart Energy

Universal Heart Poem
from the High Heart

I AM Heart Energy

Rooting In Mother Earth

Flowering up to the Divine

I AM that I AM

BE

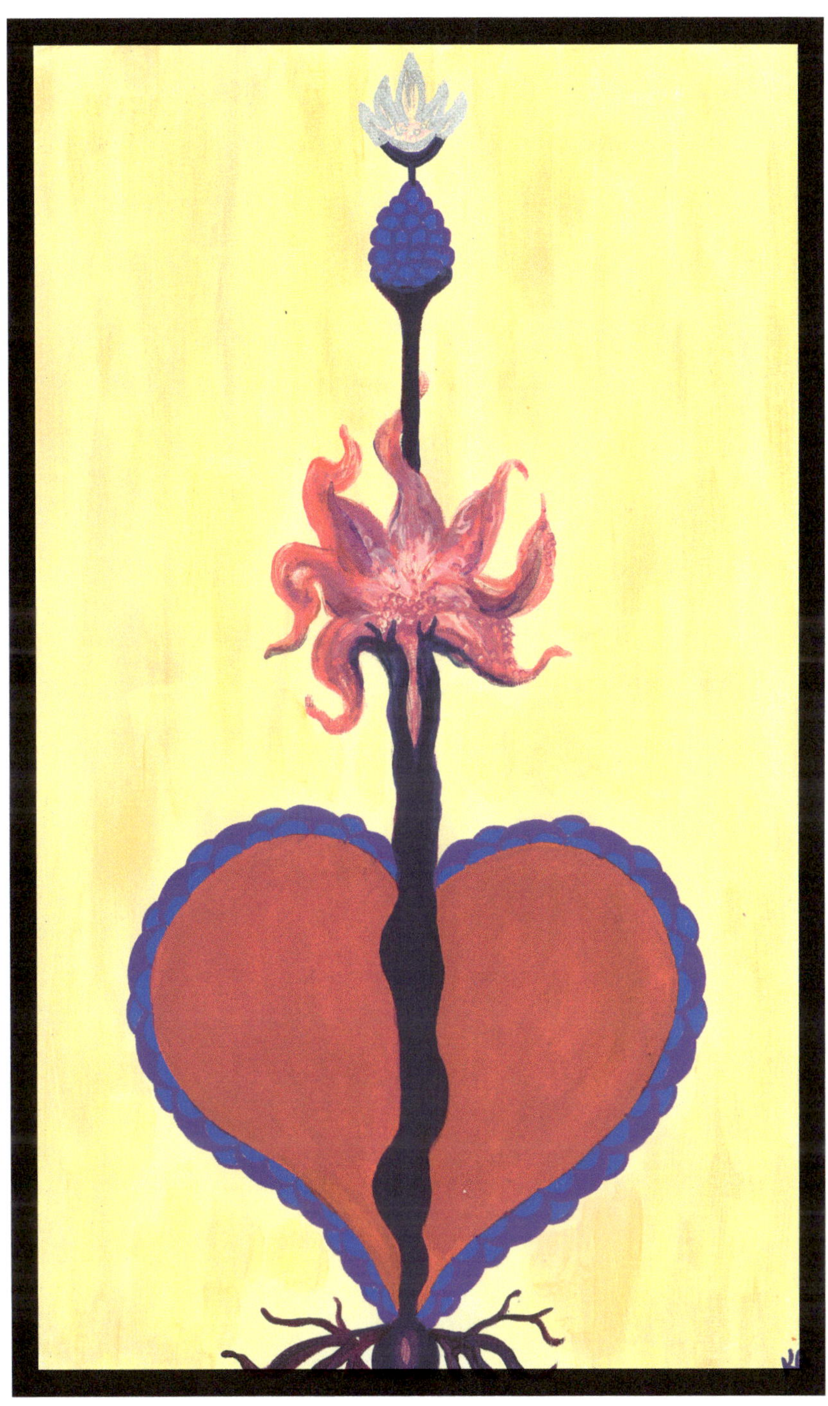

My Heart Wisdom

I AM the Heart Energy of your soul where all energy collects and then is disbursed. I AM always flowering. I AM always open. I AM always flowing. It is up to you to feel me, know me, open to me, allow me. In this physical form you are Master of my flow. I ask you to allow me, open to me, use me. I AM here to connect you with all life. ALL LIFE. I AM here to feed the flow of the Universal Divine High Heart. Be and hear my beat, feel my flow, know my immense love for you and all life.

4

♥

The Sacred Heart

Universal Heart Poem
from the High Heart

I Am the Sacred Flame

Which burns within your Heart.

I transform, transmute, transcend

All that is placed in this sacred temple

I AM the seat of Honor

I AM the seat of the Divine

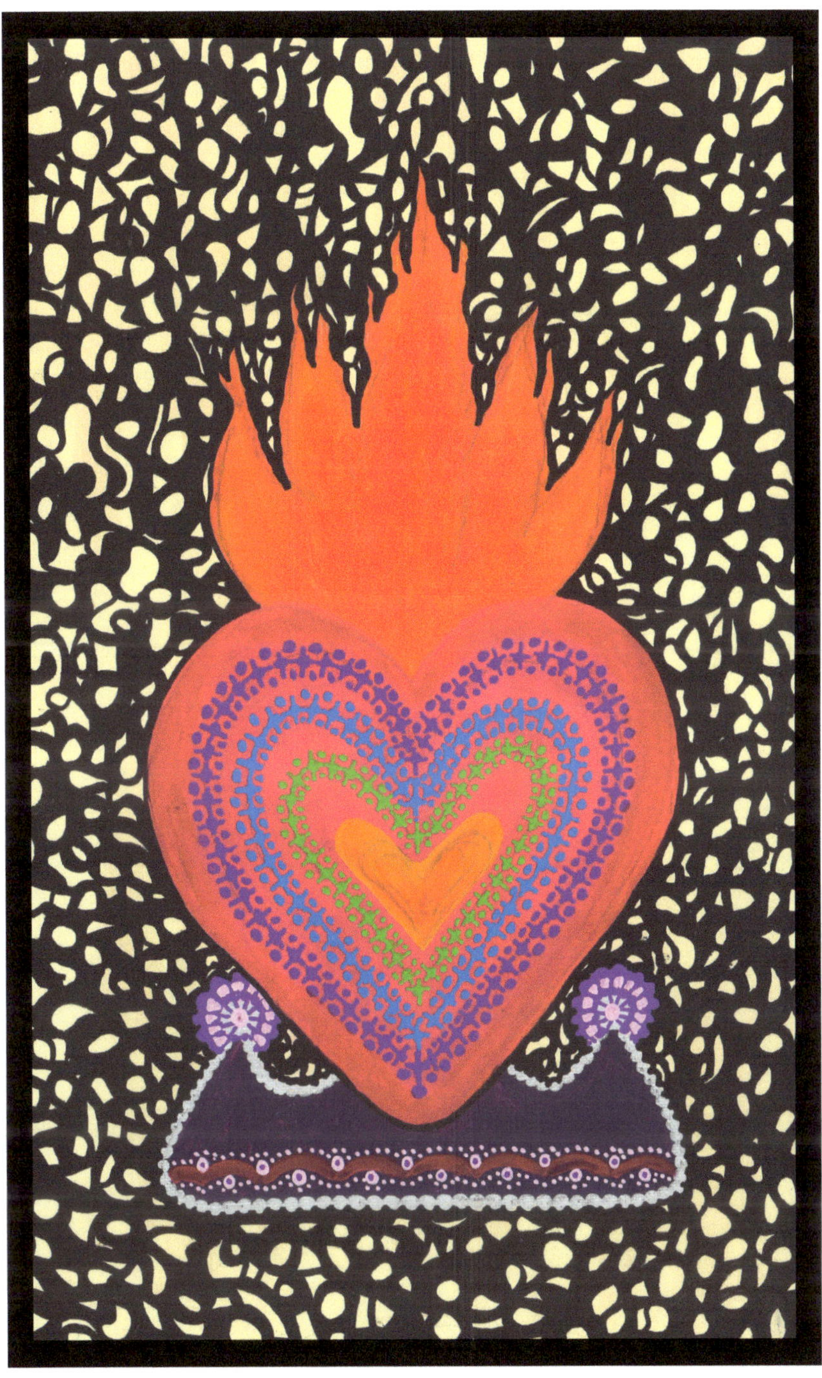

My Heart Wisdom

I AM the Sacred Heart. The Alpha and the Omega. I AM the Creatrix which consumes all. In my sacred space all transformation takes place. I destroy to bring about the truest beauty which lies within. I AM the eternal flame which burns for your transformation. Lay yourself down within my Holy Flames and feel the Divine Destruction of all that no longer is. Know my delight in the raw beauty that remains. I AM the Eternal Flame burning bright. Know my light, feel my heat. I AM within the temple of your heart. I burn for the One True Self.

5

♥

Heart Caduceus

Universal Heart Poem
from the High Heart

I AM the rising energy of Love

Healing the Heart

Flooding every cell with the light of the Divine Oneness

I sing, wings spread, songs of Love

Listen, Hear

Listen, Heart

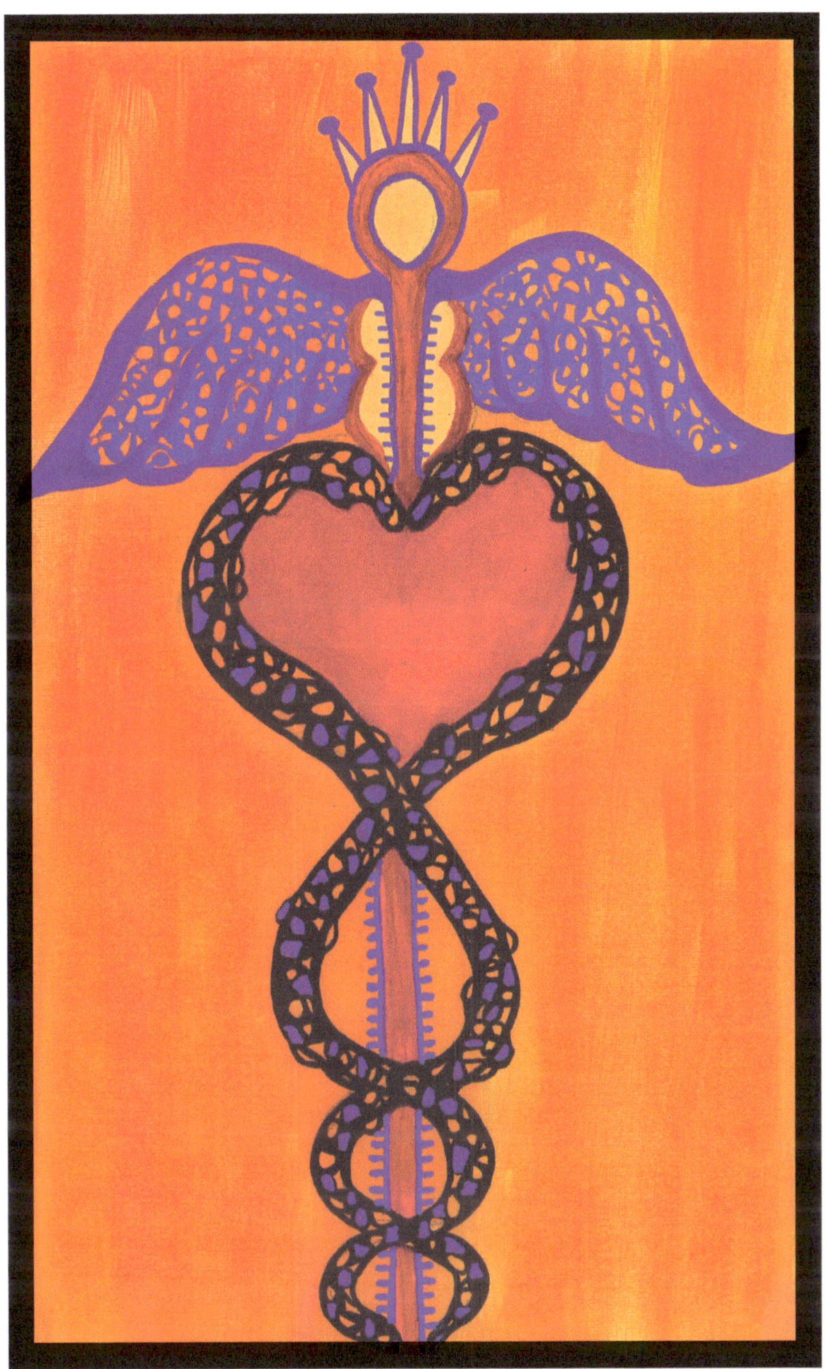

My Heart Wisdom

I AM Heart Caduceus. I AM the energy of love that flows throughout. Flow me within your body and without. I speak to you always . . . Listen. You must learn the hear me with your heart. If you ask I will always answer. Ask and receive, that is a universal law. When you ask I begin to heal all. If you listen with your heart and begin to hear with your heart you can assist me greatly. We will become one and whole healing can begin. I'm asking you to hear with the ear of your heart. This is the true meaning of healing. Hearing with the ear of your heart. Try it, Be it.

6

♥

Heart Past

Universal Heart Poem
from the High Heart

I AM Heart Past

Feeling every emotion

Everything is created by the Divine

Which always leads back to the Divine

From the Divine

To the Divine

The Circle of Life

The Flow of Life

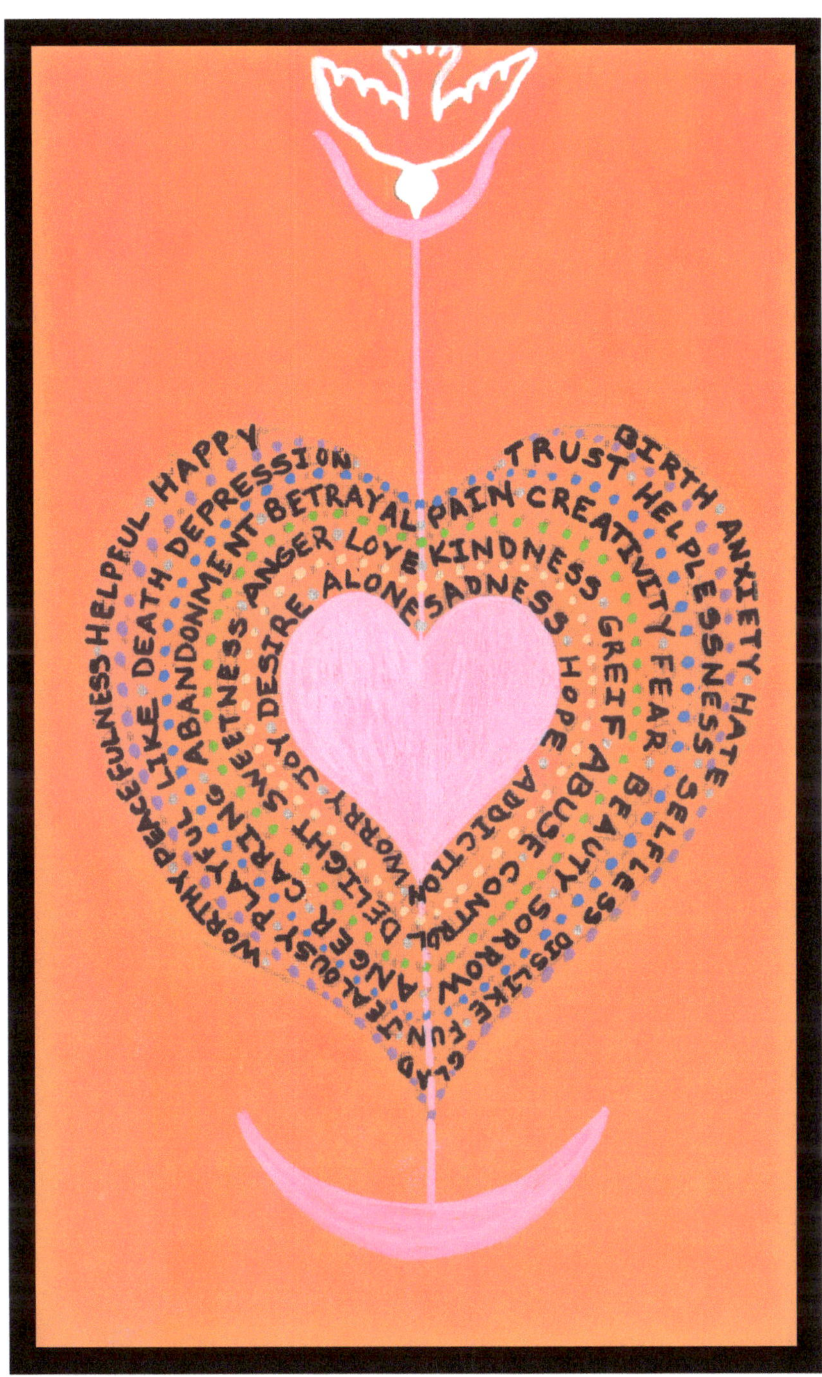

HAPPY
TRUST
BIRTH
HELPFUL DEPRESSION
ANXIETY
BETRAYAL PAIN CREATIVITY
HATE
HELPLESSNESS
DEATH
ANGER LOVE KINDNESS
SELFLESS
ABANDONMENT
FEAR
SWEETNESS
GREIF
DESIRE ALONE SADNESS
BEAUTY
PEACEFULNESS
HOPE
ABUSE
LIKE
ADDICTION
CONTROL
DISLIKE
WORRY JOY
SORROW
WORTHY
DELIGHT
FUN
JEALOUSY PLAYFUL
CARING
ANGER
GLAD

My Heart Wisdom

I AM important. Do not minimize me! I AM part of the High Heart. I AM part of the whole and felt all together I create understanding of the Oneness. Do not fear me. I AM a messenger with important words. Ask any feeling how it is helping you and the feeling will tell you. We are all here to serve the Master. And you, my dear one, are the Master. As above so below, as below, so above.

7

♥

Heart Present

Universal Heart Poem
from the High Heart

I AM Heart Present

Flowering Now

Being Now

All Is Now

Now

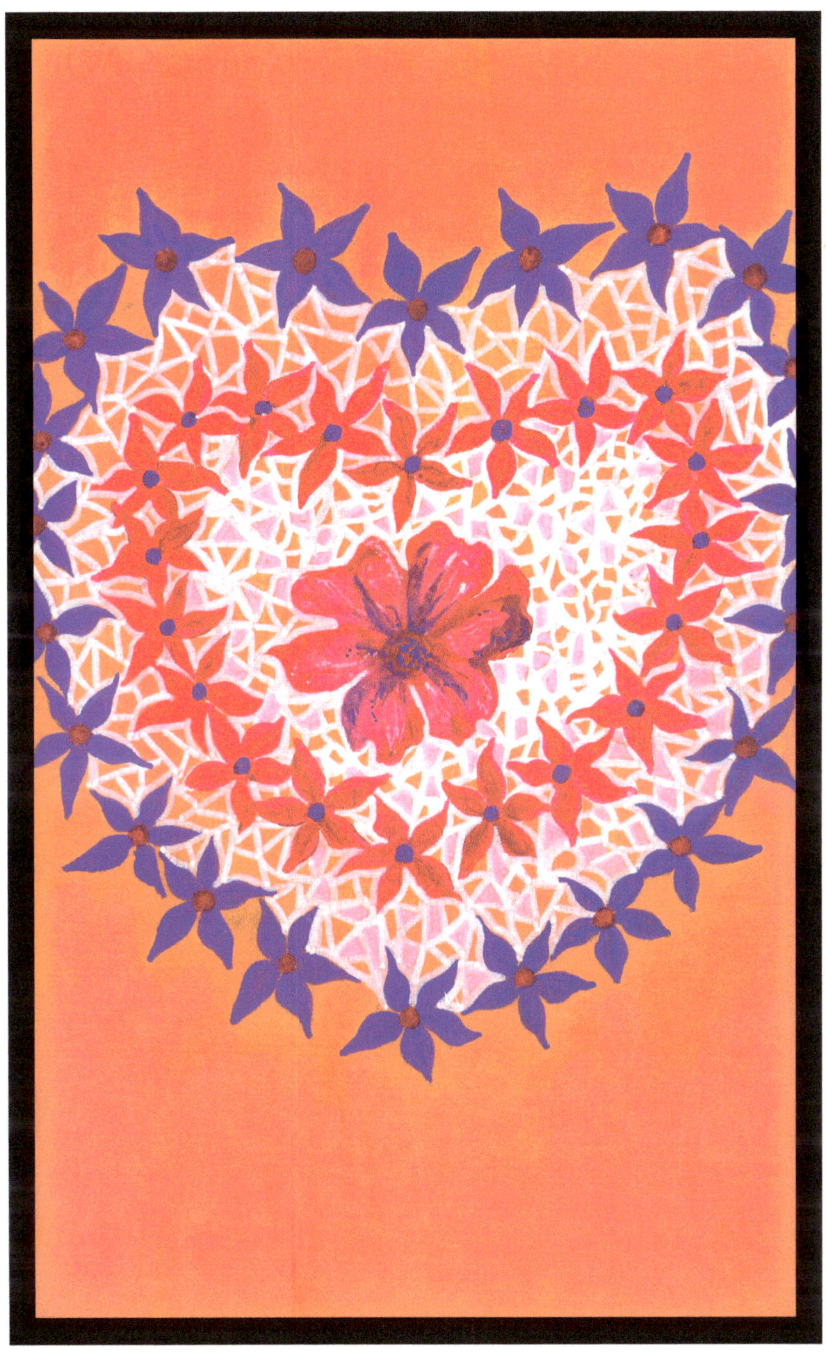

My Heart Wisdom

I AM the Now. In me time does not exist, all is now. Although it is hard to comprehend, try. All is Now. All creation, all beings (dead and alive), all places, All here now. Close your eyes and try to see. See your connection to All. Feel your connection to All. Know your connection to all people, all places, all objects. The earth calls you to people and places you know. All is Now. All is alive now in the center of the flower. You can access it any time through the center of the flower. The Heart Center is the portal of Now.

8

♥

Heart Future

Universal Heart Poem
from the High Heart

I AM the Way

Follow your Heart

It guides you to Me always

Live in the Heart and there you shall rest in Me.

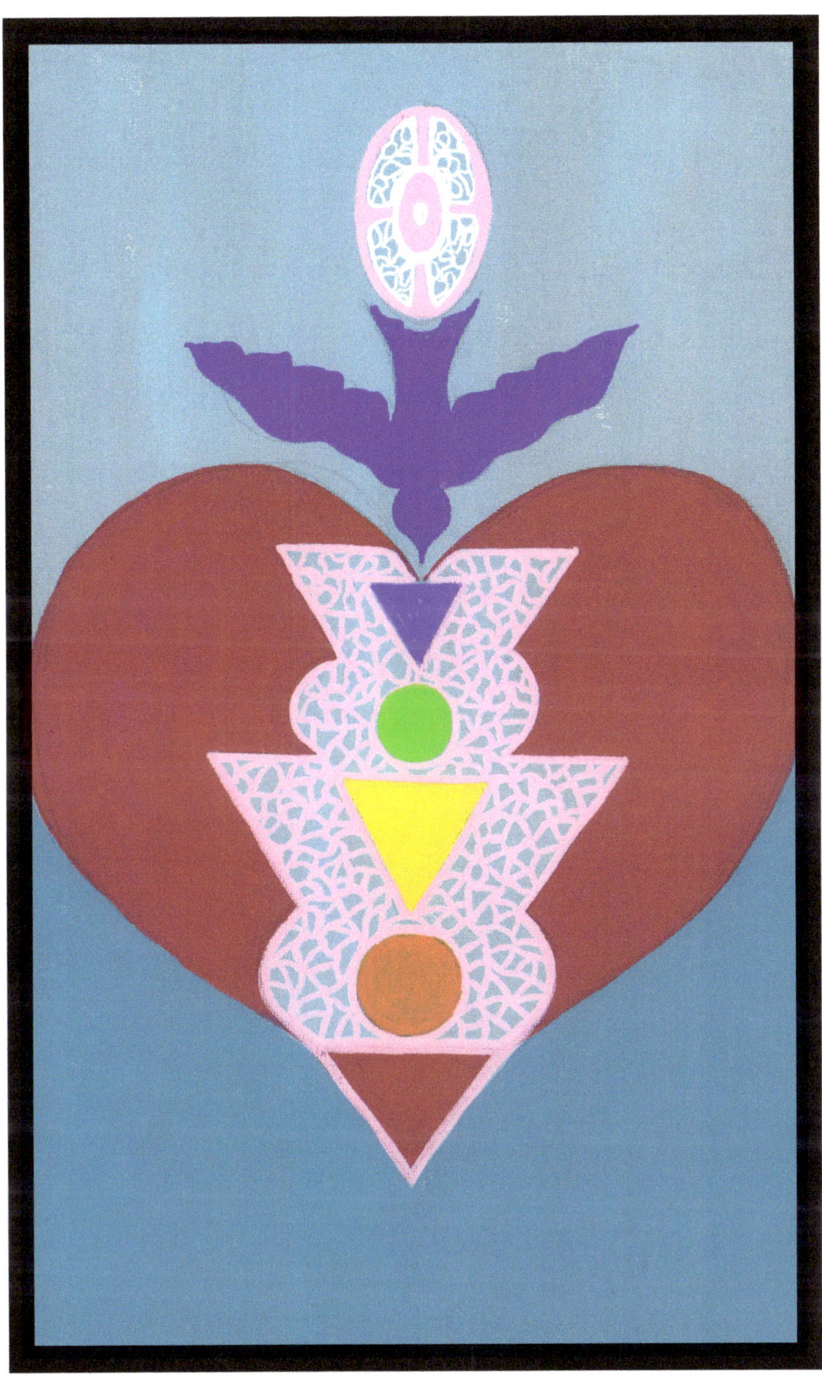

My Heart Wisdom

Words cannot convey the meaning. Your heart speaks in symbols which carry the energy vibrations which sustain you. Forget about the words for they hold very little. Look at the symbols and feel into them with your heart. See through the eye of the heart, then you shall understand. I descend into the heart and that is where I reside. Visit me there throughout your day and you will begin to reside there permanently.

9

♥

Heart Awakening

Universal Heart Poem
from the High Heart

I AM the Awakened Heart

The Heart of the Earth

The Heart of the Sky

The Heart of You

The Heart of All

I Hear All

I Feel All

I See All

I Know All

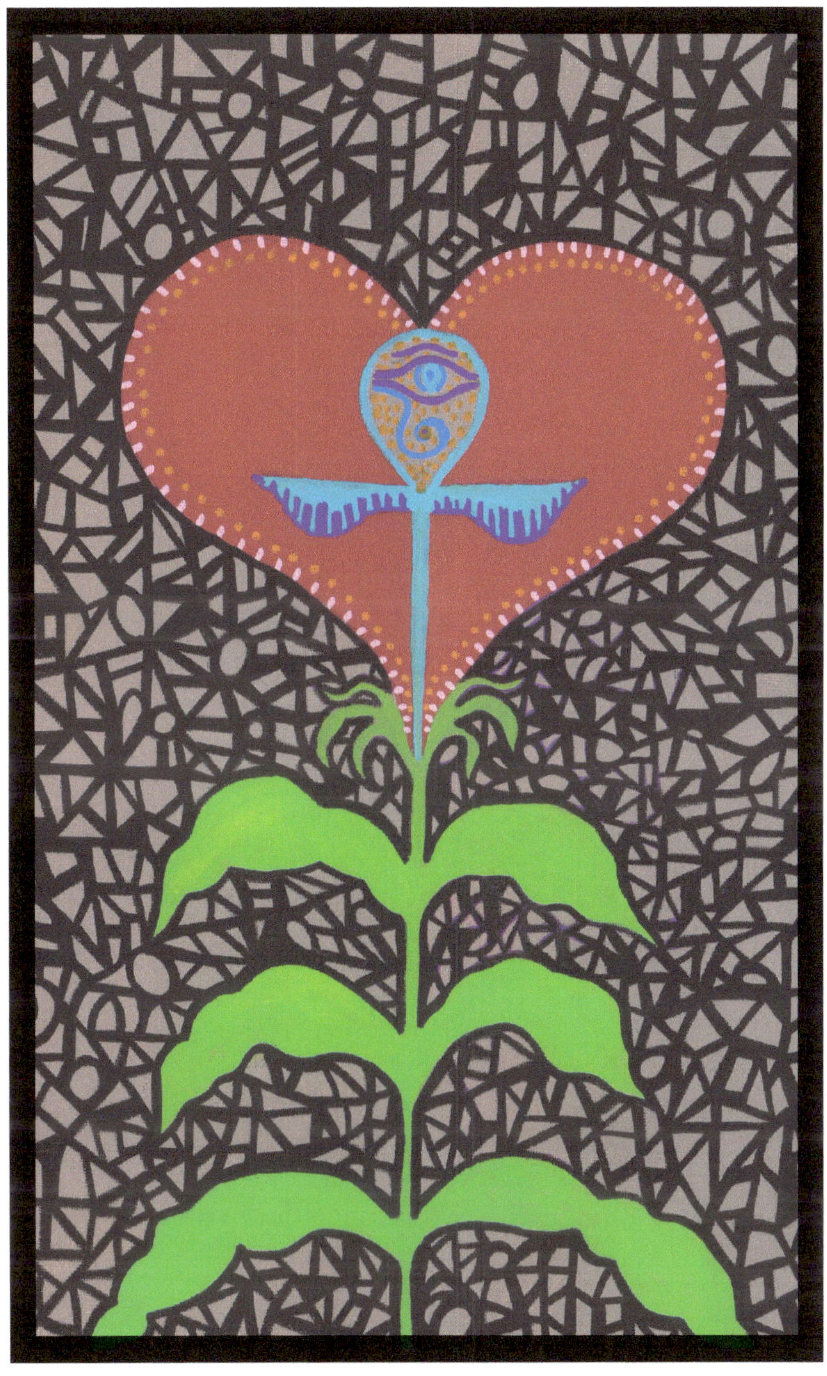

My Heart Wisdom

Look at Me. Look into my Eye. What do you see? If you look with the eye of your heart you can see into anything. You can know all. Be still and look into the eye of your heart. What do you see?

I see the sadness of this world and the suffering of the worlds beyond this time. I see the light of the world emanating from the Heart to soothe, heal and transform this suffering and sadness into a new design. A new plant which grows with stalks of joy and laughter. Changing all in it's path. Dropping new seeds on the soil and producing a New Earth on which to live. Spread the joy. Plant the laughter. Watch it grow.

.

10

♥

Heart Anchoring

Universal Heart Poem
from the High Heart

I AM the energy of Heart Anchoring

Anchor in the All Present Heart.

Filling you with light

Electrifying your field with pearl essence

Anchor in Love

Anchor through Love

Anchor as Love

Together in the Sophia Christ Conciseness.

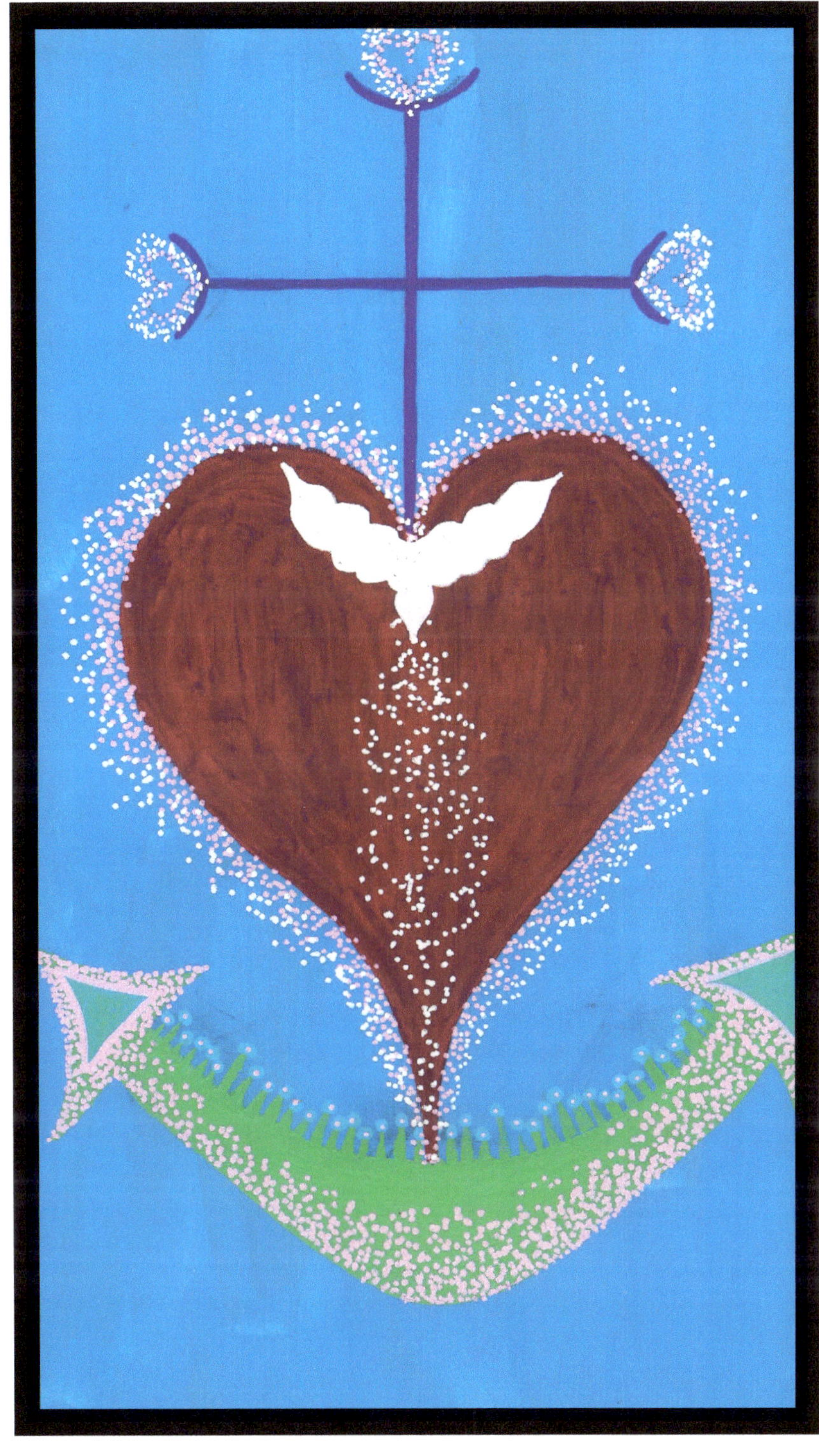

My Heart Wisdom

I have entered your heart and I have anchored the Divine Magdalene Christ energy within you. You are anchored in love, anchored through love, anchored as love. You are manifesting more and more love. As I illuminate, so shall you. As I love, so shall you. Stay anchored, stay centered in your heart. Whenever you feel unbalanced, go to your heart space and anchor deeply. There you shall always find peace and clarity.

.

11

♥

Heart Home

Universal Heart Poem
from the High Heart

I AM Heart Home

The Divine resting place of the Trinity

I descend on the wings of the Dove

Uniting the energy flow into the prefect Triad

Be One in Three

Be One in ME

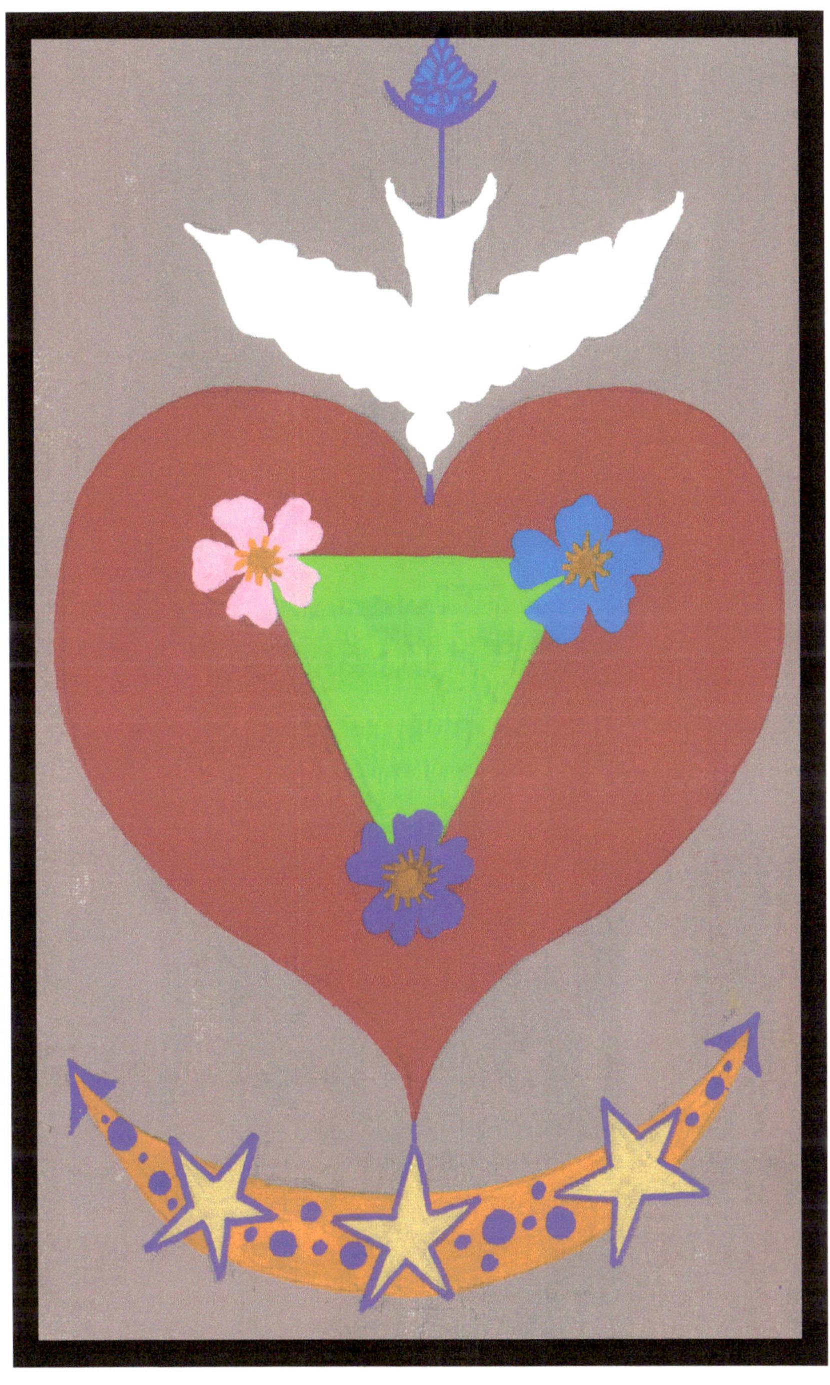

My Heart Wisdom

I AM your long awaited home. The one you have been searching for so long. You have arrived safe and sound. Rest in me sweet one, I AM here. Stay, make yourself an alter, sit and be with Me. Rest in my loving embrace. Be energized by my radiance, adorned in my beauty. Be at home always in your beloved Heart Home, where the three become one in love.

12

♥

Universal Heart

Universal Heart Poem
from the High Heart

I Am the Universal Divine Heart containing the love of the

universe

Feel your Heart expanding as you gaze upon Me

I Am entering your Heart

Feel Me Expand

Know my Love

Feel my Joy

Forever we are One

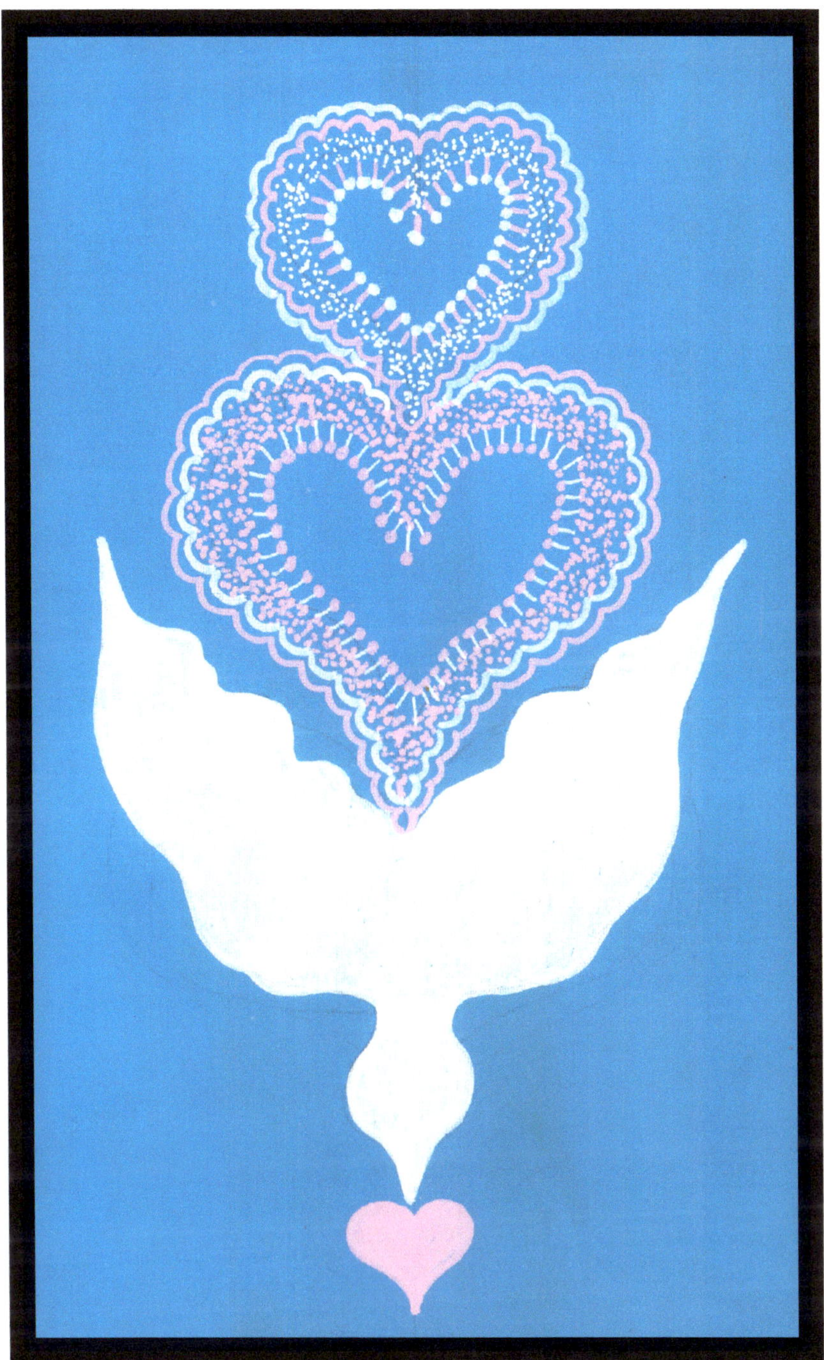

My Heart Wisdom

I AM the Universal Heart, the Heart which contains all Hearts! I am the beginning and the end and within me all is created. I am the unlimited void containing unlimited joy, unlimited sorrow, unlimited possibilities. Yours is to touch, to explore, to search the depths of Me. I AM the container which holds All. I AM—know me in all and through all you create. It is why you do create—to know me, to touch me, to explore me within and without.

.

Acknowledgments

I wish to acknowledge Dawna Memont who assisted me
in the birthing of this book. Jonathan Weinert who assisted
me in the publishing of this book. The amazing tribe
of women in my life who inspire me daily (you know who
you are!). Trish and Larry for your love and support. My
heart/home family Sarah, James and Josh for holding
the space in love. My son Noah for his acceptance, love
and support. My sisters and my brother who have helped
me greatly on this journey. To all my guides, teachers,
mentors and friends along the path who have inspired me
and enriched my life, I am grateful. To my High Heart—
thank you!

About the Artist

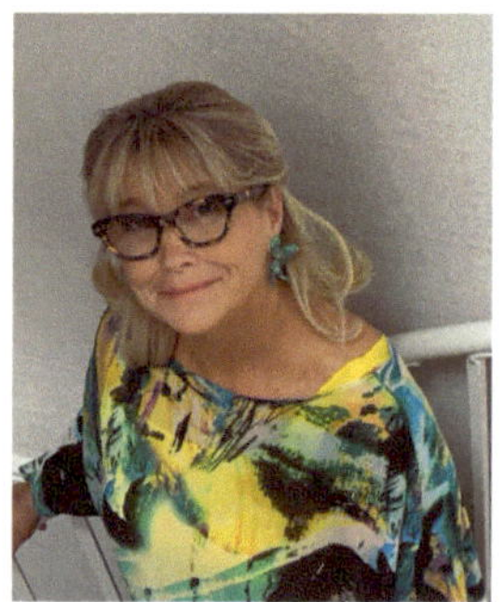

Kathleen Quigley is a working artist inspired by the beauty of nature and travel. You can view more of her work at kathleenquigley.com.